Hans-Günter Heumann

Piano Junior

A Creative and Interactive
Piano Course for Children

Theory Book 2

ED 13812

Illustrations by Leopé

SCHOTT

Mainz · London · Berlin · Madrid · New York · Paris · Prague · Tokyo · Toronto

ED 13812
British Library Cataloguing-in-Publication Data.
A catalogue record for this book is available from the British Library
ISMN 979-0-2201-3638-2
ISBN 978-1-84761-429-2

English translation: Schott London Editorial
Design by Barbara Brümmer
Typesetting Elke Göpfert
Music setting: Darius-Heise-Krzyszton
Cover design: www.adamhaystudio.com
Printed in Germany S&Co. 9207

Contents

Summary of Lesson Book 2

Intervals

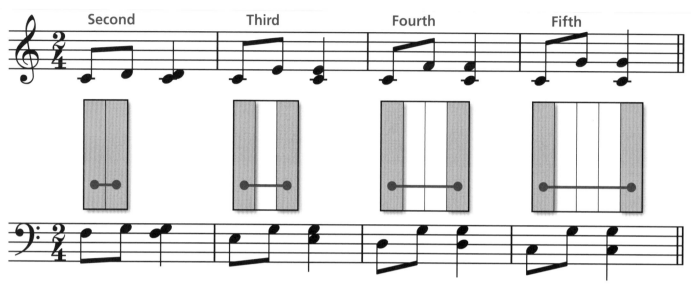

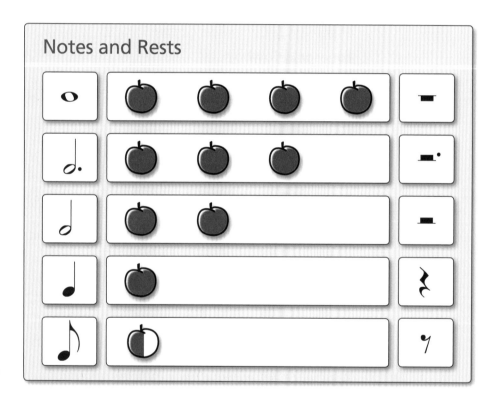

Dotted Crotchet/Quarter note

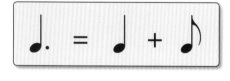

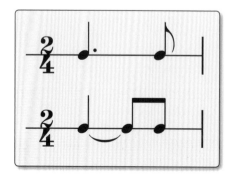

Musical Terms

C = 4/4

- marcato
- poco a poco
- dolce
- maestoso

- Adagio
- Allegretto
- Presto

- rall./rit./ritard.
- dim./dimin.
- decresc.
- cresc.

- A-B-A / Ternary form

♯

♭

♮

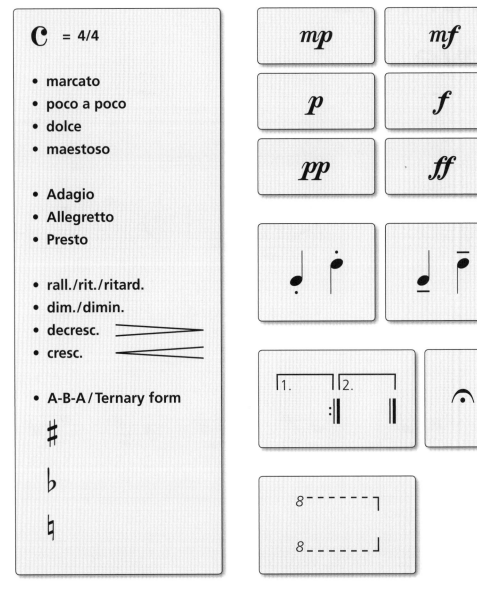

mp *mf*

p *f*

pp *ff*

Range of Book 2

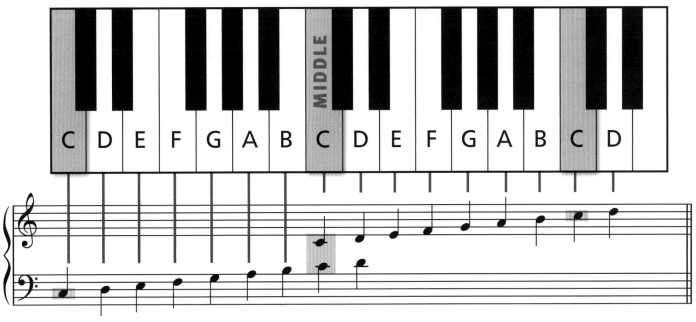

C D E F G A B **C** (MIDDLE) D E F G A B **C** D

5

Writing Intervals on the Stave

Second
distance of 2 notes

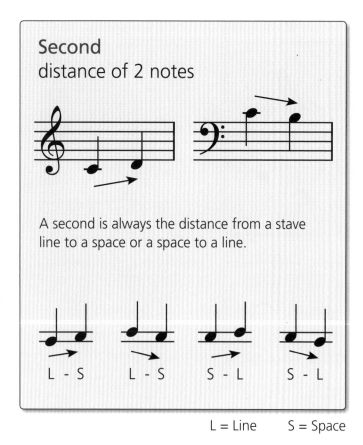

A second is always the distance from a stave line to a space or a space to a line.

L - S   L - S   S - L   S - L

Third
distance of 3 notes

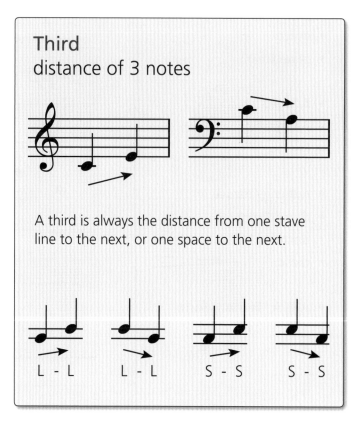

A third is always the distance from one stave line to the next, or one space to the next.

L - L   L - L   S - S   S - S

L = Line   S = Space

Fourth
distance of 4 notes

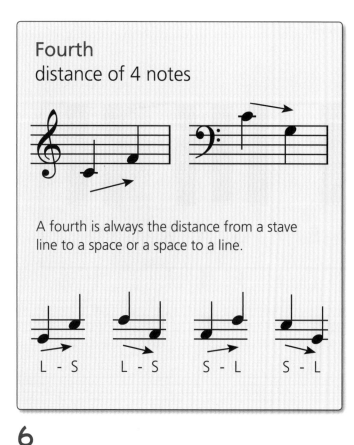

A fourth is always the distance from a stave line to a space or a space to a line.

L - S   L - S   S - L   S - L

Fifth
distance of 5 notes

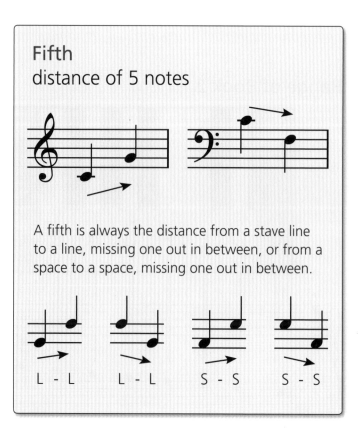

A fifth is always the distance from a stave line to a line, missing one out in between, or from a space to a space, missing one out in between.

L - L   L - L   S - S   S - S

Name and write these Intervals

Second ↗ _____

Third ↘ _____

_____

Fourth ↑ _____

_____

Fifth ↗ _____

_____

_____

Love is Everywhere

Pop Ballad

HGH

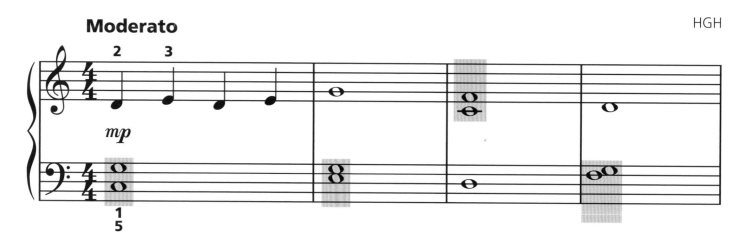

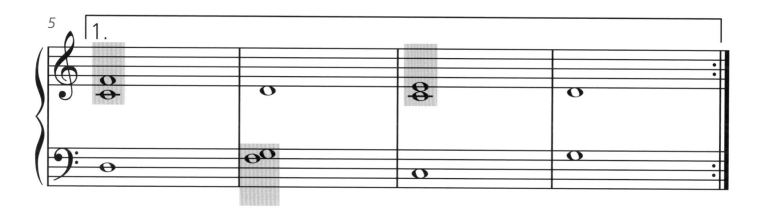

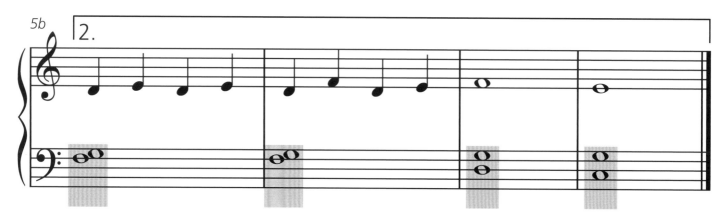

Play Harmonic Intervals Melodically

Love is Everywhere

Pop Ballad

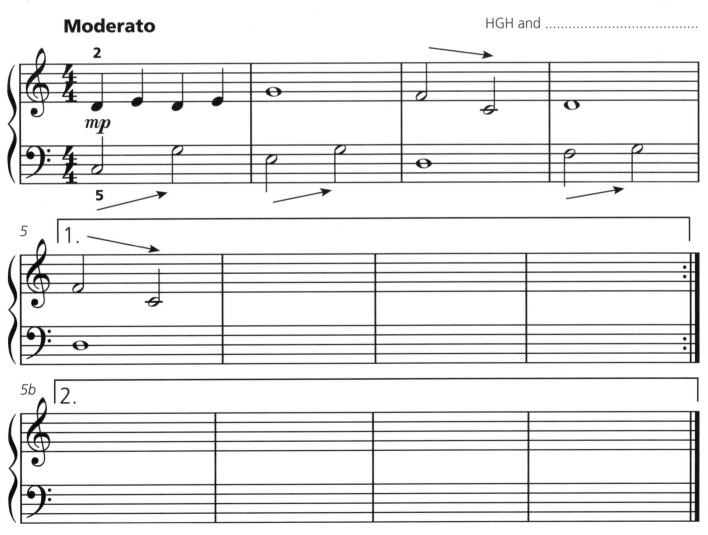

Upbeat

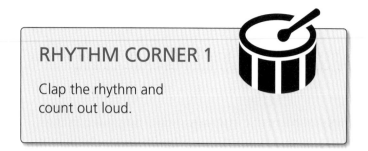

One note is missing from the last bar. Fill it in.

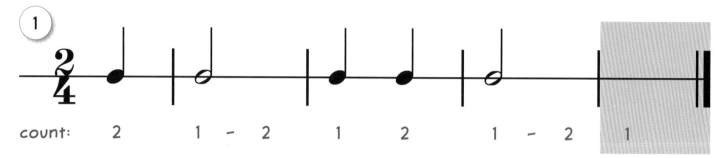

A note is missing from the upbeat. Fill it in.

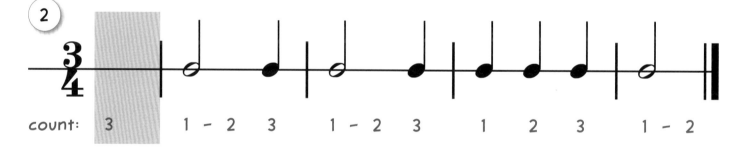

In this exercise notes are missing from the upbeat and the
final bar, but which ones? Fill them in.

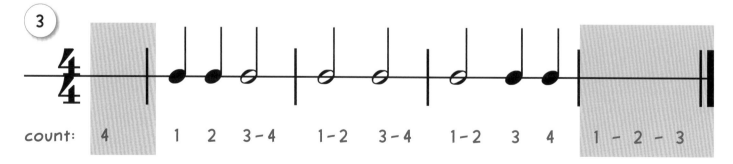

Musical Pictures

IMPROVISING CORNER

Draw a picture in the space below and set it to music on the piano. Think about what the picture might sound like. For instance, to portray an elephant, long notes, played slowly would sound good to give an impression of its slow walking pace. However, high notes, played loudly, would also be fantastic for the trumpeting of the elephant. Perhaps your teacher will play other musical pictures for you. There are no limits to your imagination.

Have fun!

Seven White Keys Feel – Touch – Play

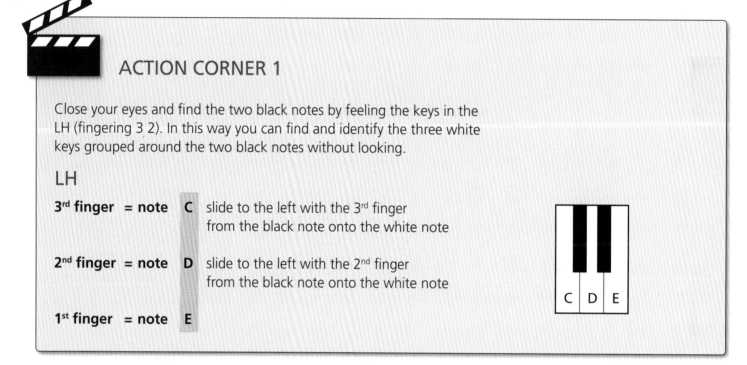

ACTION CORNER 1

Close your eyes and find the two black notes by feeling the keys in the LH (fingering 3 2). In this way you can find and identify the three white keys grouped around the two black notes without looking.

LH

3rd finger	= note	**C**	slide to the left with the 3rd finger from the black note onto the white note
2nd finger	= note	**D**	slide to the left with the 2nd finger from the black note onto the white note
1st finger	= note	**E**	

Close your eyes and find the three black notes by feeling the keys in the RH (2 3 4). In this way you can find and identify the four white keys grouped around the three black notes without looking.

RH

1st finger	= note	**F**	
2nd finger	= note	**G**	slide to the right with the 2nd finger from the black key onto the white key
3rd finger	= note	**A**	slide to the right with the 3rd finger from the black key on to the white key
4th finger	= note	**B**	slide to the right with the 4th finger from the black key on to the white key

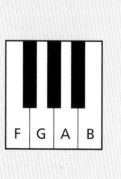

Rests

RHYTHM CORNER 2

Clap the rhythms and count out loud.
Observe the rests – don't clap here, but hold the hands apart.

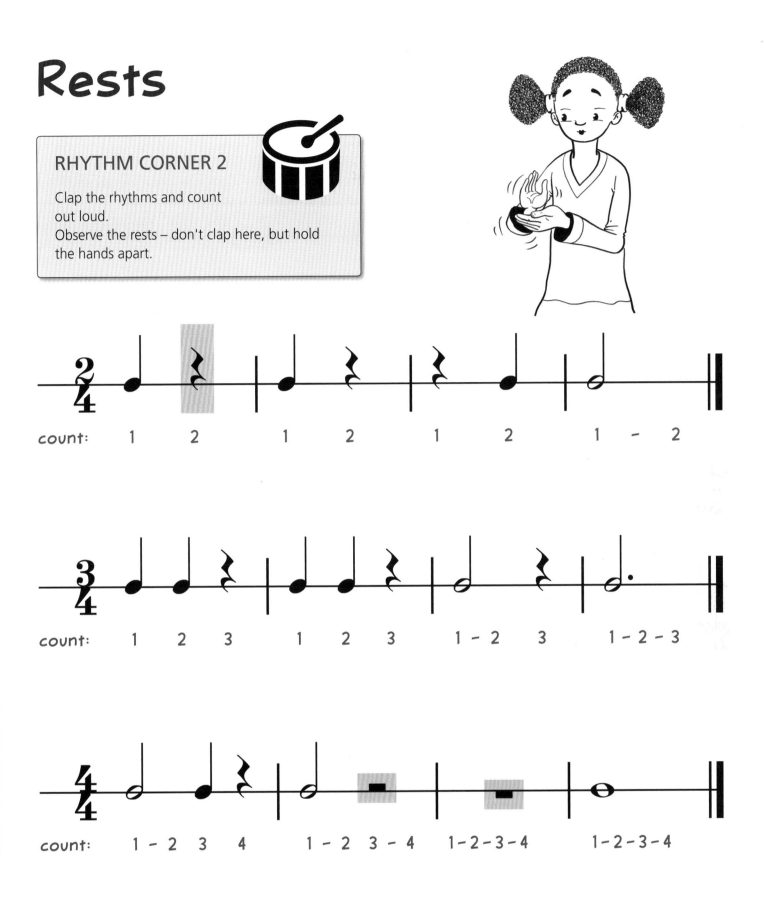

count: 1   2   1   2   1   2   1 – 2

count: 1   2   3   1   2   3   1 – 2   3   1 – 2 – 3

count: 1 – 2   3   4   1 – 2   3 – 4   1-2-3-4   1-2-3-4

Compose a Melody

COMPOSING CORNER 2

Below you will see the notes to be used in the RH and LH. In the piece, the RH rhythm is given above the stave and notated for the LH on the stave. Compose a nice melody and write it down on the stave. Think of an appropriate name for your piece. Why not memorize this piece and perform it to an audience?

Notes to use

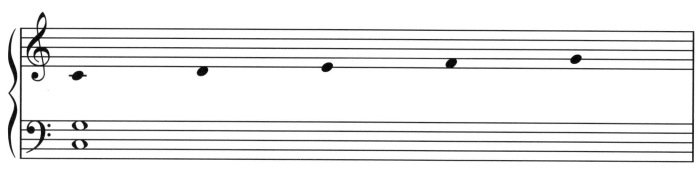

....
Title of the piece

composed by: ....

....
Tempo

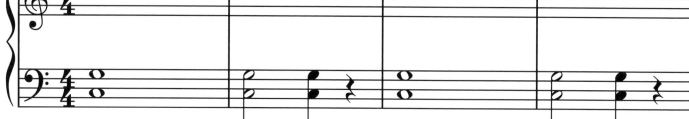

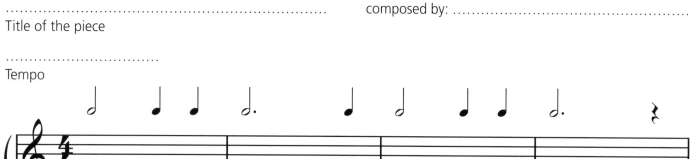

Brain Teaser

The Sad Clown

The Siren

Happy Waltz

Singing Hippopotamus

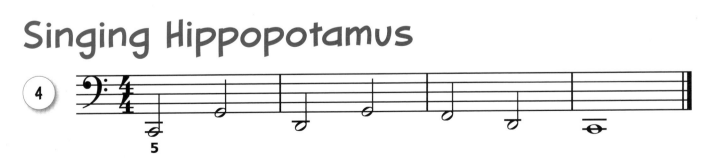

Turn Me Upside Down

ACTION CORNER 2

If you turn the book upside down the notes and key signatures look exactly the same. Try it! Magic! Draw in the clefs, brackets and notes, using the dotted lines as a guide. Also add the missing notes.

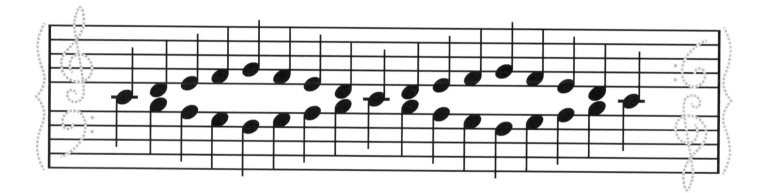

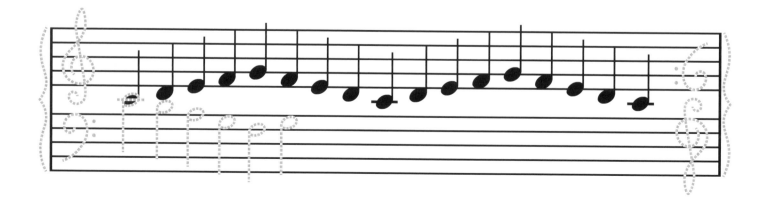

The Mirror Image

COMPOSING CORNER 3

Write a second part, in the bass clef, in mirror image to the melody given below.
This is like a question and answer game and is great fun!

Mirror, Mirror on the Wall ...

Moderato

HGH and ....

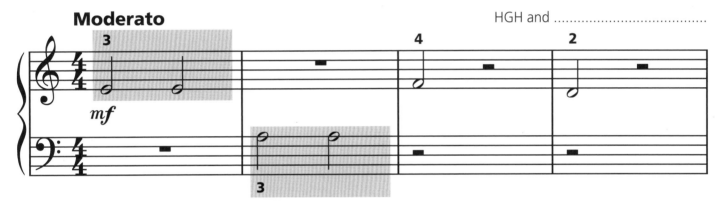

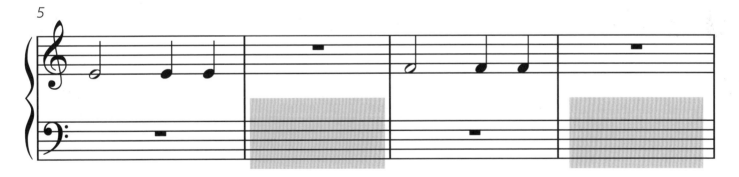

Sing and Play Along!

La La La

EAR TRAINING CORNER 1

Sing this melody with and without the help of the piano. Then play the accompaniment with the LH and sing the melody La La La.

RH: Melody

HGH

La la la la la la la, la la la la la,_____

la la la la la la la, la la la la la._____

LH: Accompaniment

18

Quaver/Eighth Note

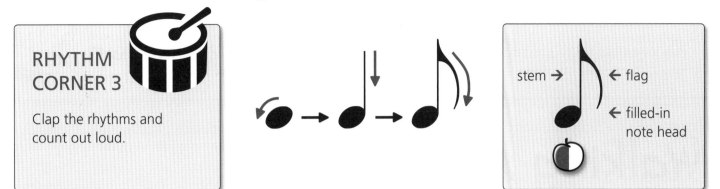

RHYTHM CORNER 3

Clap the rhythms and count out loud.

stem → ← flag

← filled-in note head

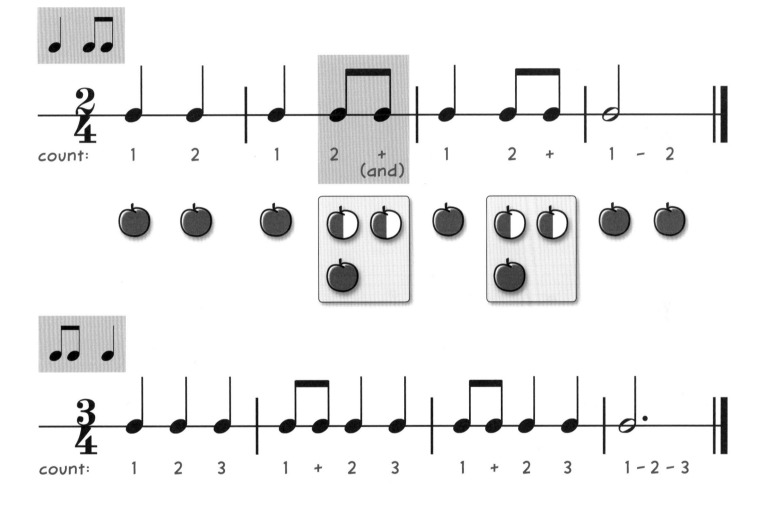

count: 1   2   1   2   +   1   2   +   1 – 2
                            (and)

$\dfrac{3}{4}$

count: 1   2   3   1   +   2   3   1   +   2   3   1 – 2 – 3

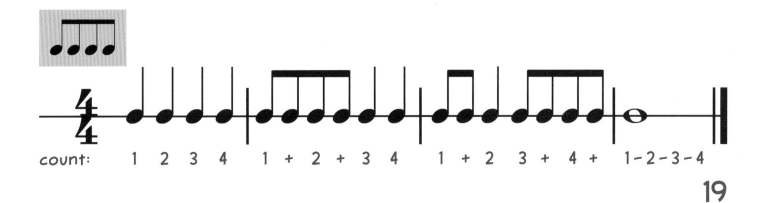

$\dfrac{4}{4}$

count: 1 2 3 4   1 + 2 + 3 4   1 + 2 3 + 4 +   1 – 2 – 3 – 4

Changing the Time

Play WALKING ALONG first in 4/4 time as notated. The piece is then changed into 2/4 and 3/4 time. Fill in the missing notes and then try playing everything.

COMPOSING
CORNER 4

Walking Along

Andante

German Folk Song

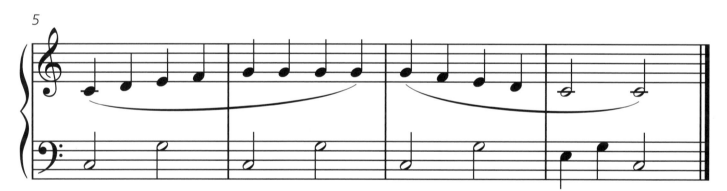

Walking Along

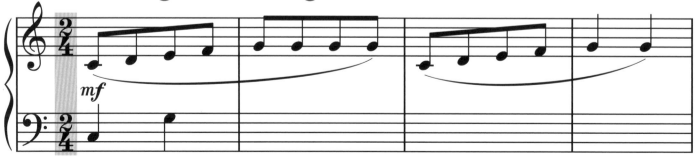

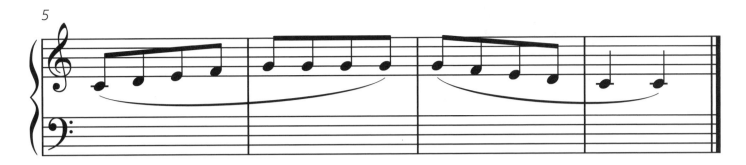

Walking Along

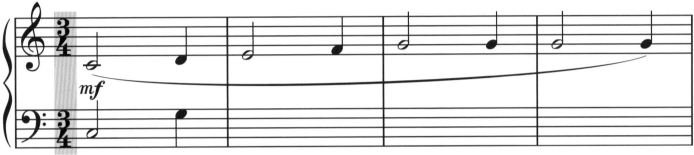

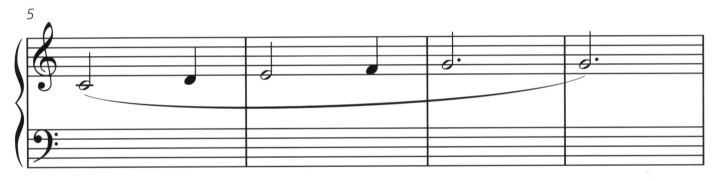

Notes in the Treble Clef

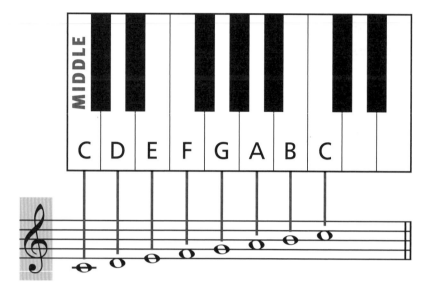

Write the notes as semibreves/whole notes, minims/half notes, crotchets/quarter notes and quavers/eighth notes.

22

Notes in the Bass Clef

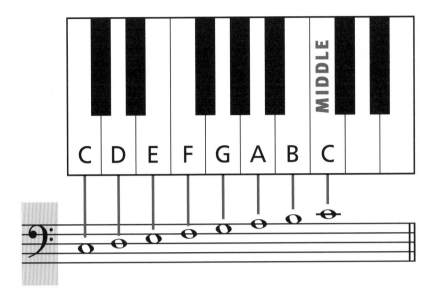

Write the notes as semibreves/whole notes, minims/half notes, crotchets/quarter notes and quavers/eighth notes.

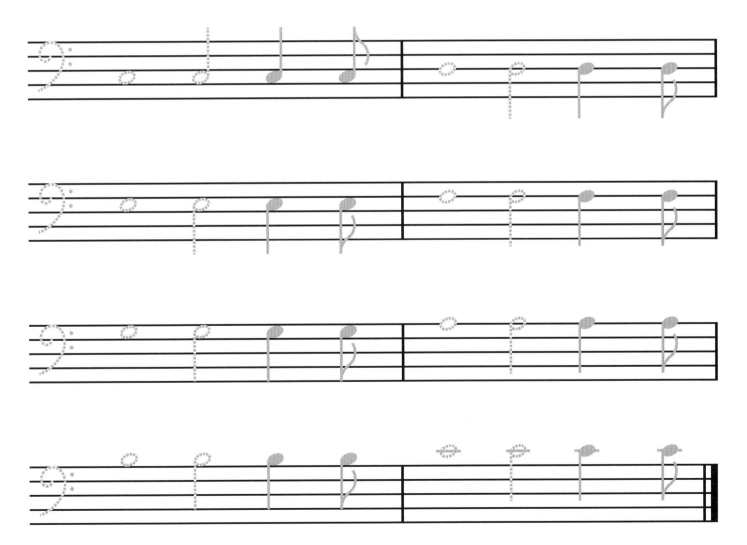

Sight-Reading

You have a little time to look at each new piece before playing it. Always look at the most important things first. For example: the clef, time signature, starting note with fingering, dynamics, rhythm and shape of the music

Play slowly, without hesitation, even if you make a mistake. Make sure your eyes are on the music, rather than the keys. Off you go!

SIGHT-READING CORNER

HGH

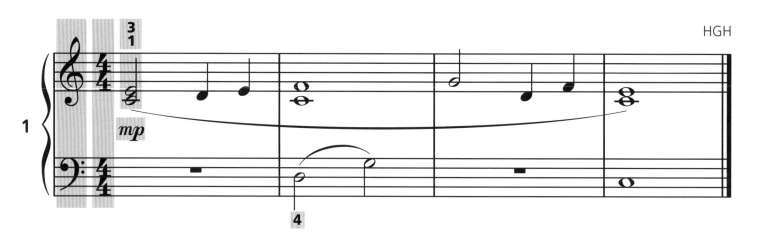

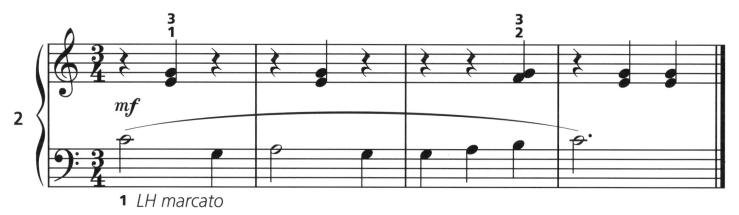

1 *LH marcato*

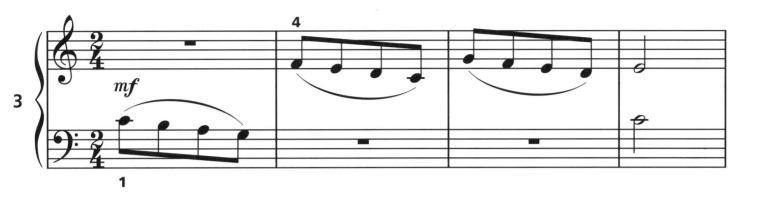

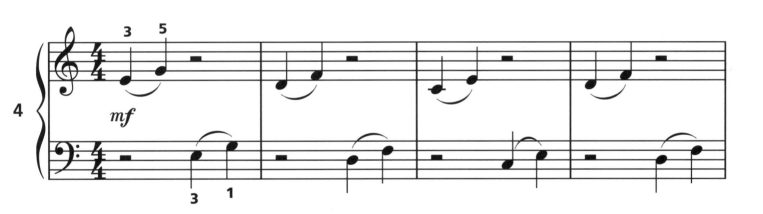

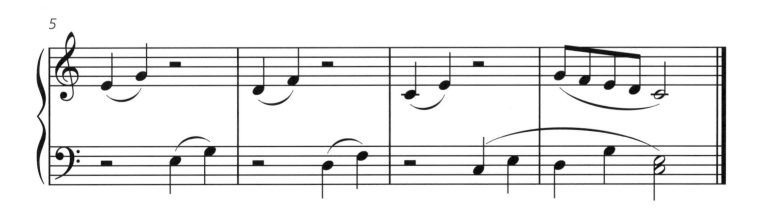

25

Piano Piece with Variation

Moderato

HGH

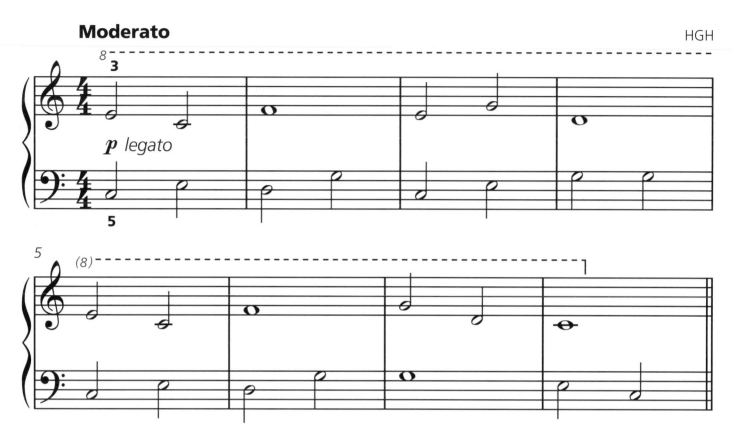

Variation

In the Variation, the melody has been altered slightly, but the accompaniment stays the same. The notes marked in red indicate the original melody, which appears in the Variation with exactly the same rhythm. Practice with the RH alone, concentrating on emphasizing the melody notes.

Variation

Variation

Name these Notes

My First Chamber Music Piece

Your first chamber music piece lets you play along with another instrument. Perhaps you have a friend who plays the flute, the violin, or sings? Have fun together!

By the way, **chamber music** means music for just a few musicians rather than a piece for a large orchestra.

Banks of the Ohio

American Folk Song
Arr.: HGH

Allegretto

mp I asked my love ___ to take a walk, ___ to take a walk, ___

just a lit - tle walk. ___ Down be - side ___ where the wat - ers

flow, ___ down by the banks ___ of the O - hi - o. ___

Intervals

Your teacher will play the intervals for you, on the piano, melodically and harmonically in any order. Just listen the first time, sing along the second time, and the third time you should sing the intervals alone, without support of the piano. After this, you should name the interval. Try to identify the leaps by filling in the steps. So for a fourth, sing the second, then the third, and finally the fourth.

1. Listening Test

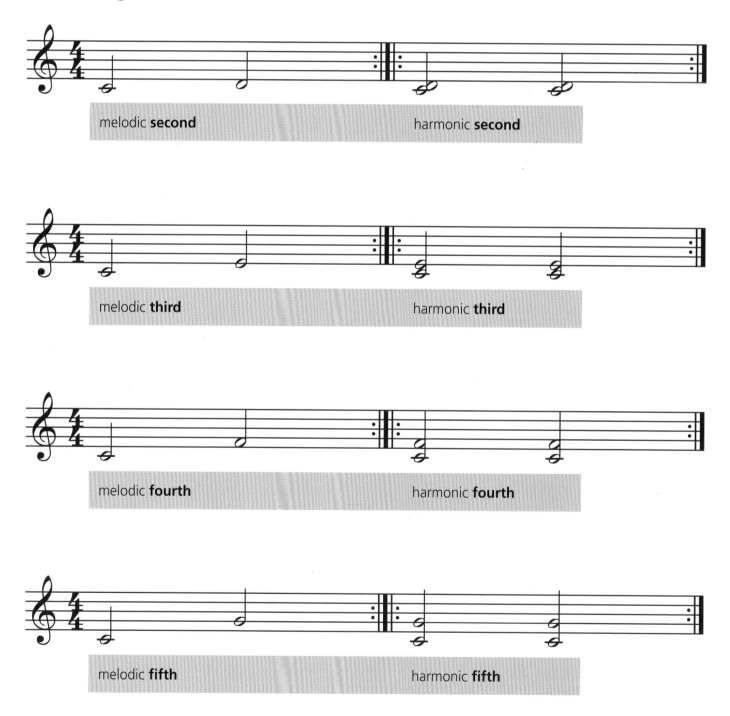

melodic **second**　　　　　harmonic **second**

melodic **third**　　　　　harmonic **third**

melodic **fourth**　　　　　harmonic **fourth**

melodic **fifth**　　　　　harmonic **fifth**

2. Sing the Exercises

Sharp Sign ♯

Lonesome Cowboy

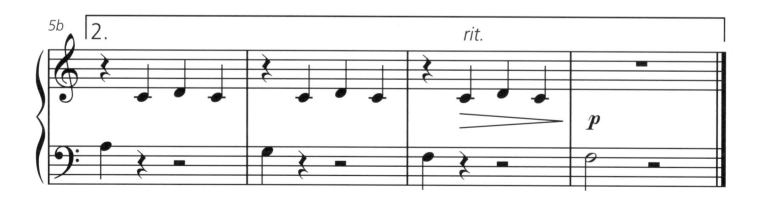

Play LONESOME COWBOY on page 32 a semitone higher. For this the piece is notated in the same way, but sharp signs are added before each note. The fingering is the same, so you should be able to play this piece right away.

COMPOSING CORNER 5

Lonesome Cowboy

Andante

HGH and ....

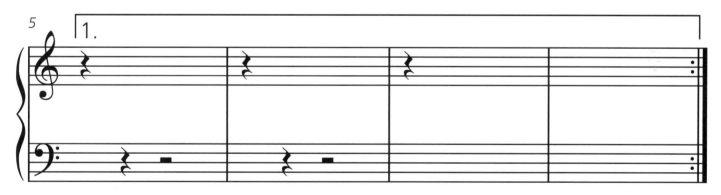

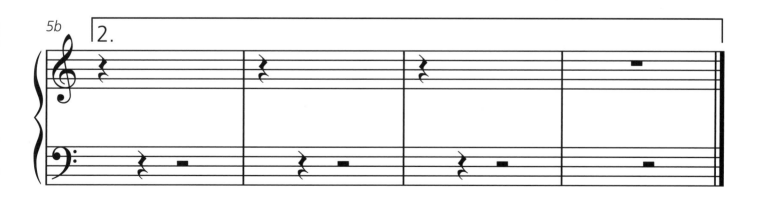

Walking in the Mist

HGH

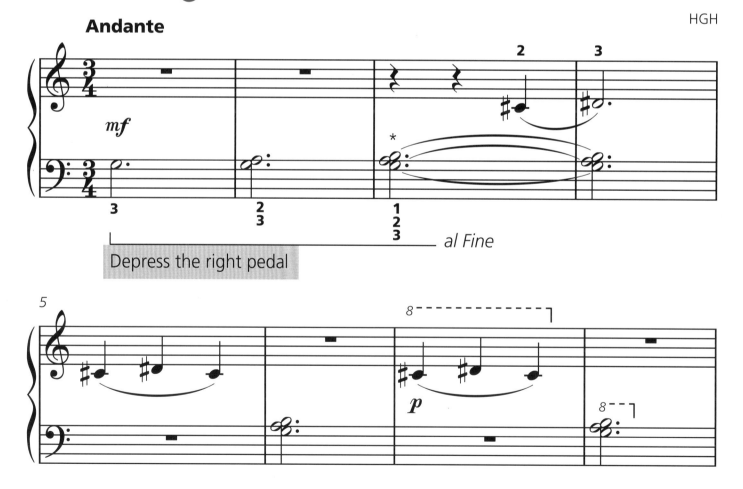

Depress the right pedal

al Fine

*) A **cluster**, or note cluster, describes several notes grouped very close to one another. On the piano, several neighbouring notes are played at the same time (see also pages 36–39).

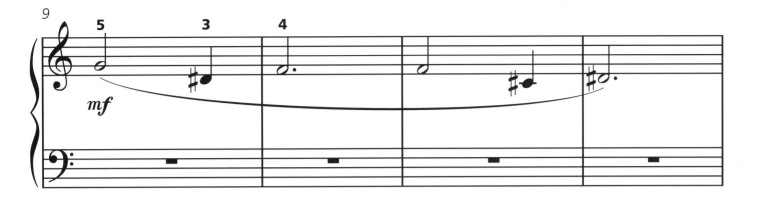

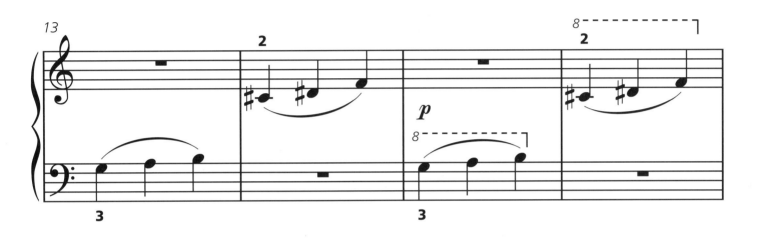

Flat Sign ♭

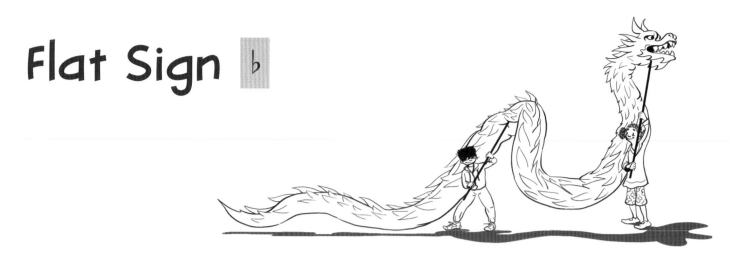

Chinatown Waltz

Allegro

HGH

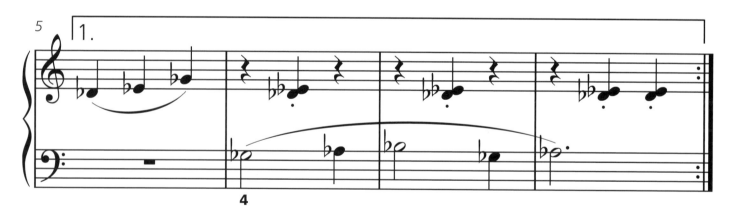

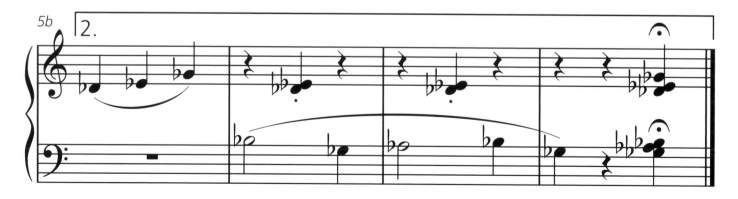

If you play the two versions of CHINATOWN WALTZ, you will notice that they sound exactly the same although they are notated differently. The note names are also different. For example, the first note on the left-hand page is D flat and on the right-hand page it is C sharp. There are therefore two names for each note, one with flats and one with sharps.

PLAYING CORNER 2

Chinatown Waltz

Allegro

HGH

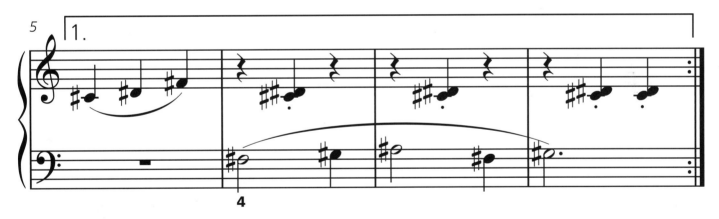

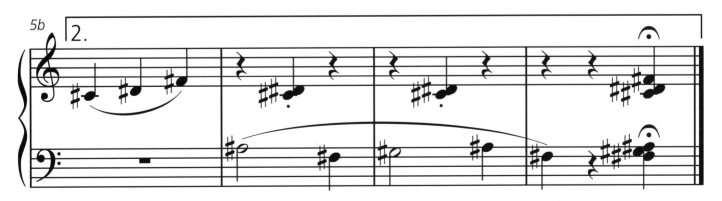

Rain and Thunderstorm

Presto

HGH

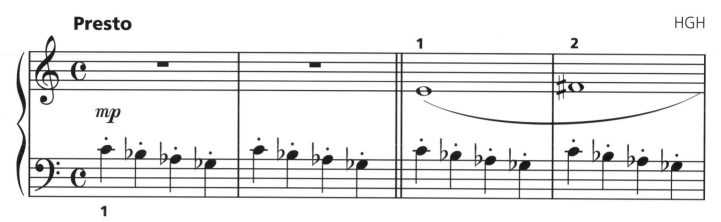

38

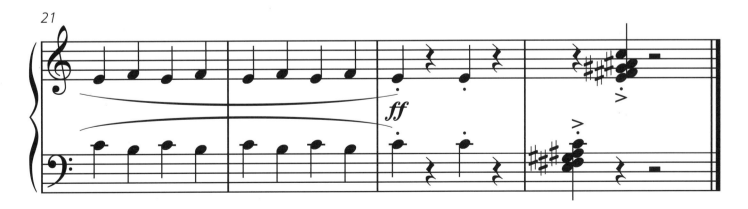

Name these Notes

Dotted Crotchet/ Quarter Note ♩.

RHYTHM CORNER 4

Clap the rhythm and count out loud.

count: 1   2 +
            (and)

1 - 2 +   1 - 2 +   1 - 2

count: 1   2 + 3   1 - 2 + 3   1 - 2 + 3   1 - 2 - 3

count: 1   2 + 3 - 4   1 - 2 + 3 - 4   1 - 2 + 3 - 4   1 - 2 - 3 - 4

42

Echoes

Andante

HGH

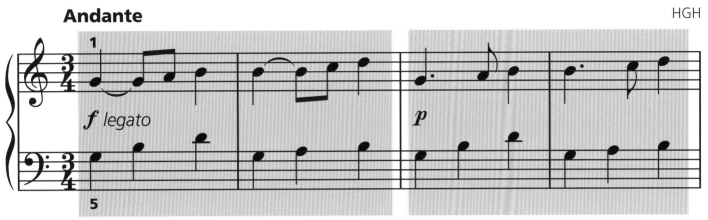

LH marcato

Another Chamber Music Piece

The Circus is Coming

45

Piano Junior Quiz

1. What is the name of an interval whereby the notes are played one after another?

☐ a) harmonic interval
☐ b) melodic interval
☐ c) rhythmic interval

2. What is the name for the distance of 4 notes?

☐ a) Second
☐ b) Fifth
☐ c) Fourth

3. What is the term for the musical form with A-B-A themes?

☐ a) Variation form
☐ b) Two-part form
☐ c) Ternary form

4. Which bar should be added to the upbeat to make a complete bar?

☐ a) Final bar
☐ b) Penultimate bar
☐ c) Second bar

5. What is the name of this rest ?

☐ a) crotchet/quarter note rest
☐ b) minim/half note rest
☐ c) semibreve/whole note rest

6. Which of these indicates a slow tempo?

a) allegretto

b) allegro

c) moderato

d) adagio

7. What does the term *crescendo* mean?

a) getting slower

b) getting quicker

c) getting louder

d) getting quieter

8. What is the term for playing short and detached notes?

a) staccato

b) legato

c) tenuto

9. Which sign raises the note by a semitone?

a) ♭

b) ♯

c) ♮

10. Which is the correct way of indicating increasing dynamics from very quiet to very loud?

a) *pp - p - mf - mp - f - ff*

b) *pp - mp - p - mf - f - ff*

c) *pp - p - mp - mf - f - ff*

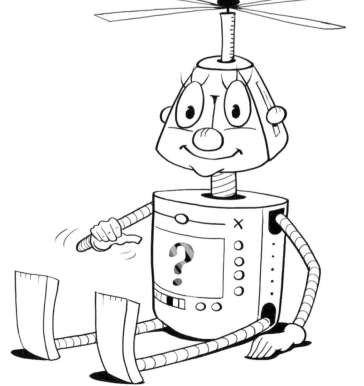